Foote, Lucius Harwood, Hubbard Elbert

On the Heights

a Volume of Verse

Foote, Lucius Harwood, Hubbard Elbert

On the Heights
a Volume of Verse

ISBN/EAN: 9783743311947

Manufactured in Europe, USA, Canada, Australia, Japa

Cover: Foto ©Thomas Meinert / pixelio.de

Manufactured and distributed by brebook publishing software
(www.brebook.com)

Foote, Lucius Harwood, Hubbard Elbert

On the Heights

CONTENTS—Concluded
TRANSLATIONS

Serenade	111
Rosette	112
Carmen	113
To	114
Remembrance	115
Dedans Paris	117
Let Them Dream	118
Childe Harold	120
Song	120
From the Barricades	121

Something more than the lilt of the strain,
  Something more than the touch of the lute;
For the voice of the minstrel is vain,
  If the heart of the minstrel is mute.

ON THE HEIGHTS

ON THE HEIGHTS.

"The rock fell under us in one sheer sweep, thirty-two hundred feet."

HE CRAWLS along the mountain walls,
From whence the severed river falls;
Its seething waters writhe and twist,
Then leap, and crumble into mist.
Midway between two boundless seas,
Prone on a ragged reef he lies;
Above him bend the shoreless skies,
While helpless, on his bended knees,
Into that awful gulf profound,
Appalled, he peers with bated breath,
Clutches with fear the yielding ground,
And crouches face to face with death.
The fearful splendor of the sight
Begets in his bewildered brain
A downright torture of delight,
The very ecstasy of pain.
A sudden frenzy fills his mind,
If he could break the bonds that bind,
And launch upon the waves of wind;
Only to loose his hold and leap,
Then, cradled like a cloud, to sleep
Wind-rocked upon the soundless deep.

With eyes upturned, he breaks the spell,
And creeps from out the jaws of hell.
Pohono's siren wiles beguile—
He drinks her kisses in the wind,
He leaves the nether world behind .
Up, and still upward, mile on mile,
With muffled tramp, the pilgrim creeps
Across the frozen winding-sheet,
Where white-faced death in silence sleeps.
Up, and still upward, to the light,
Until at last his leaden feet
Have mocked the eagle in its flight.
Grim-browed and bald, Tis-sa-ack broods
Above these white-robed solitudes.
A mute, awe-stricken mortal stands
Upon the fragment of a world ;
And, when the rifted clouds are curled,
Sees far below the steadfast lands.

♣

A FACE.

I MET a maiden on the street,—
I knew another long ago ;—
And as she passed with tripping feet,
I looked, and lo !
I saw a face I used to know.

The winsome smile, so rare and sweet,
The downcast eyes, the cheeks aglow ;
Ah me, it made my old heart beat,
Though well I know
That on her grave the daisies grow.

TYPES.

THE new and the old,
The dross and the gold,
The chaff and the wheat
Commingle and meet,
Here, where the banners of sunset are furled
On the rim of the world.
New forms and new faces
Confront the old races,
And challenge the scions of Saxon descent.
Such a wonder, to-day,
On the crowded highway,
Flashed on my sight for a moment, and went.
Like the Goddess of Dawn,
With the step of a fawn,
And lithe as a leopard, she passed, and was gone.
Her sire is a Celt, and her mother was born
Where the bountiful light of a Tuscan morn
Falls on the billows of ripened corn.
Escutcheons are nothing to her, although
One ancestor fought under Cæsar in Gaul,
And another went down by the bastion-wall,
When Sidney, at Zutphen, was slain by the foe.
Though her marvelous face, with its halo of hair,
Is so hauntingly fair,
There's a smoldering fire which flickers and flashes
Beneath her lashes,
And the ghost of an old Patrician disdain,
Like the phantom of pain,
Is lurking now
In the swell of her nostril, and shade of her brow.
In fine,

15

There is pride and passion in every line,
From her finger tips,
To the arch of her foot, and the curve of her lips.
Men have gone to their death, for women like this,
And counted it bliss.
In the hush of her chamber, this very night,
She will tell her beads in the chastened light,
And pray to the Mother of God to keep
Her soul in sleep.
Ah me,
Both saint and sinner is she—
But who can tell what the end will be?

♣

WAITING.

I HEAR his footstep on the stair,
　　My heart responds with quickened beat,
As to my ear the sound-waves bear
　　The eager accent of his feet.

O heart! my heart, canst thou gainsay
　　The hope that echoes in his tread;
He comes to woo and win to-day,
　　To-morrow he may come to wed.

THE WOOING OF THE ROSE.

A WHITE rose bloomed in a garden close,
  On a tristful autumn day;
Sad was the heart of the fair white rose,
  As the summer slipped away.

She had been wooed by the singing bird,
  The bee and the butterfly;
But never a chord of her heart was stirred,
  Till she heard the west wind sigh.

She leaned on the trellis, fair and sweet,
  With the laughing leaves above,
As he glided in with his noiseless feet
  And whispered his tales of love.

A rollicking, restless rover, he—
  The waif of the salt-sea brine,
And only a white, white rose was she,
  The last of her royal line.

He kissed the lips of the rose in bloom,
  And alas, a-lack a-day!
She was despoiled of her rare perfume,
  For the wind will have its way.

VIGNETTES.

I.

I HAVE somewhere the sketch of a cottage
   home,
   With the sunlight flooding the humble
   room;
While the south wind tosses the mottled foam
   Of the orchard boughs in their bloom.

Under trailing roses a maiden stands,
   Demurely sweet in her simple guise;
A quiet grace in her folded hands,
   And a world of faith in her eyes.

She dreams the dear dreams of youth and of hope,
   Of a knight who is coming from over the sea—
Of a fairy castle on wooded slope,
   Of the lover that is to be.

II.

With suitors in waiting on either hand,
   A proud dame watches the tide as it flows.
Minerva in marble is not more grand,
   Than is she in her cool repose.

Her make-up, a marvel of pink and of pearl;
   Self-poised, she turns in her conscious grace—
From the braided coils of her hair a curl
   Falls over the billows of lace.

Or she sits at her ease and calmly smiles,—
   Her lord has been dead for a year and a day,—
Weaving the web of her well-bred wiles
   In a nonchalant, listless way.

18

ENVOY.

Time is a worker of wonders; I knew
   Both the artless maid and the stately dame;
And strange indeed, as it seems the two
   Were verily one and the same.

✿

SHAKESPEARE.

THE years, O Bard! add lustre to thy name;
   We hail thee, wonder of a wondrous age;
   And when high art portrays thy peopled
      page,
We see, as London saw, with loud acclaim,
Macbeth take counsel of his haughty dame,
   The Hunchback storm across the mimic stage,
   The Moor, made mad with passion, vent his rage,
And fat Jack Falstaff vaunt his deeds of shame.
The men, begotten in thy peerless brain,
   Are types of hero, villain, braggart, fool;
Thy women, women to the very core.
For thy rare counterpart we seek in vain;
   Seer of no sect, and helot of no school,
Reign thou in high Parnassus evermore.

WHEN RICHARD LOVELACE CAME TO WOO.

THE feet of time make fast apace,
　　And we, like players in a play,
Strut up and down our little space,
　　And act our parts as best we may;
Alas! Alack! and well-a-day!
The stage is dight in somber hue,
Where once that stately vogue held sway,
　　When Richard Lovelace came to woo.

And much we marvel, as we trace
　　The feuds and foibles passed away;
While pomp of power, and pride of place
　　Troop down the years in grand array.
In court and camp, in fete and fray,
Fickle and flippant, staunch and true,
　　Such were the gallants, bold and gay,
When Richard Lovelace came to woo.

In doublet fine, and frills of lace,
　　The lover sought his suit to pay;
With such a form and such a face,
　　Who could resist his plea, I pray;
And then that tender roundelay,
So like a wood-dove's plaintive coo,
　　Sweet Lucy could not say him nay,
When Richard Lovelace came to woo.

ENVOY.

Ho, Kentish Towers! your lordly race
　　Had swords to draw, and deeds to do,
In that eventful Year of Grace,
　　When Richard Lovelace came to woo.

20

GUIDO.

I KNOW you are fair,
But what do I care
For the lustre of eyes
And the ripple of hair.
The earth is forlorn, and the heavens are lead ;
Since under the arch of the pitiless skies,
Guido, brave Guido, my brother lies dead.
Together we three,
That is, Guido and I,
And the mother who bore us,
Lived in a cottage that looks on the sea ;
The mountains behind, and the glad waves before us,
And over us ever the blue of the sky.
We breasted the deep in the gray of the morning,
And mended our nets at the ebb of the tide ;
And we laughed,
And we chaffed,
At the fond mother's warning,
Who could not forget how our good father died.
Thus peacefully speeded
The seasons unheeded,
Till rumors were rife
Of the roar of the battle and din of the strife ;
There was call for the lovers of country to come,
And Guido grew restless, I knew what it meant,
He was life of my life, and together we went ;—
Oh ! her eyes were so dry and her lips were so dumb,
As we marched away,
At the break of day,
To the blare of the trumpet, and beat of the drum.
It was grand to rally for freedom and God ;

21

But, oh the ruin, and oh the cost;—
We conquered the foe, but the battle is lost,
Since Guido, dear Guido, lies under the sod.
The red lights flash forth from the red-tiled town,
And the brazen tongues of the bells ring out,
And the men and women go up and down,
And meet us,
And greet us,
With cheer and shout;
But a mother stands watching beside the door,
While the spent waves moan on the shingly shore.

O SLY BO-PEEP.

O SLY BO-PEEP! behind a chair,
I catch a glimpse of tangled hair,
    And laughing eyes and dimpled cheek;
    Then comes a challenge, faint and weak,
As if to lure me to thy lair.

With loud pretense, I wonder where,
Behind what door, upon what stair,
    And hear, when found, thy joyous shriek;
                    O sly Bo-Peep!

In after years, grown passing fair,
When hearts, perchance, are in the snare,
    Pray tell what games of "hide and seek,"
    Wilt thou provoke in pet or pique,
Until Love comes to find thee there;
                    O sly Bo-Peep!

MARIE.

I T CHANCED that I, in years gone by,
Sought out one day, I scarce know why,
 The market of Aubette;
And I saw there a maiden fair,
With midnight eyes and golden hair,
 And fate and I had met.

I went again somehow, and then
I often went; for when, oh when,
 Will heedless youth beware?
The sweet surprise within her eyes,
As when the morn lights up the skies,
 Allured me unaware.

Her timid glance did so entrance,
That I, beguiled thereby perchance,
 Deemed it a mere caprice;
Ah well-a-day, how quickly may
We fritter golden hours away,
 Which promise joy and peace.

An attic high, against the sky,—
Affaire d' amour—a fragile tie—
 Two swallows neath the eaves.
One hour ago I sought and lo!
No birds were there; the one, I know,
 Has gone, the other grieves.

Dear lost Marie, I would not see
The heaven of love in store for me;
 But turned with pride away.
So now I weep, and sadly keep
My mournful vigils o'er the sleep
 Of her I spurned that day.

23

Could I forget I would, and yet,
Remorse is keener than regret,
  Requiting pain with pain.
So when the bells ring solemn knells,
I hither bring sweet immortelles ;
  Dead birds come not again.

♣

FLORENCE.

ENAMORED of thy beauty, I am here,
  To find thee robed in color everywhere ;
  Spring, with her garlands woven fresh
    and fair,
Crowns thee with youth eternal, year by year.

From out thy Campanile, the bells ring clear,
  And round about Duomo's marble stair,
  Thy careless children, gay and debonair,
Make light of toil, with jocund laugh and jeer.

Across the years I scan thy stormy past,
  And mark thy dauntless stand against control ;
  With Guelph and Ghibeline in fierce array.
And though enthralled at times, by creed and caste,
  What deathless names are on thy blazoned scroll,
  While Art, triumphant, holds its tranquil sway.

SCHAMYL'S DEFEAT.

NOW Caucasus peaks were flashing
  'Neath their crowns of dazzling snow,
How turgid streams were dashing,
  As we stemmed the torrent's flow;
Where the sun of summer dances
  On the boundless steppes below,
Brightly, brightly, gleamed our lances,
  When we met the Russian foe.

O the ramp and roar of battle!
  Beat of hoof, and clash of steel—
While the volleys flash and rattle,
  And the squadrons charge and wheel;
Far and wide the hosts are scattered,
  Long and loud the cannons peal;
Now our lines are torn and shattered,
  Now our ranks recoil and reel.

Here amid the dead and dying,
  Lost and lorn, and wounded sore—
On the cold earth I am lying,
  And the night is closing o'er;
Grant, O grant a dawn of splendor,
  There beside the Caspian shore,
Where my Mitska, true and tender,
  Waits to greet her love once more.

Lo! the lurid light is creeping
  Slowly up the eastern sky,
Round and round the vultures sweeping,
  Watch the carnage from on high;
Soon the gaunt wolves will be snarling
  O'er the corpses where I lie,
Weep not, weep not, O my darling!
  For thy lover doomed to die.

25

LADY JANE.

A N OWER true tale I fain would tell
　　Of Scottish border strife,
And how an English Earl did win
　　A Scottish maid for wife.

He was the Lord of Widdington,
　　Her kinsmen were his foes,
And she was Fraser's lovely lass,
　　A bonny heather rose.

On Cheviot's flank his Lordship's troop
　　Had met the Fraser clan,
Were scattered in the headlong charge,
　　And routed horse and man.

And lost and lorn, and wounded sore,—
　　A hunted stag at bay,
But for a maid who succored him,
　　The Earl had died that day.

She hid him in the rustling corn.
　　And gave him food and rest,
The while her baffled kinsmen sped
　　Upon their bootless quest.

And in the gloaming, o'er the hills
　　She led him safe and sound,
Until he reached the border side,
　　And trod on English ground.

Long raged the fierce and bloody feud,
　　Which rent the land in twain,
And many a lady mourned her lord,
　　And many a lass her swain.

Until one morn from Teviotdale,
  The word came down the glen,
That all was lost, and Weddington
  Held Fraser and his men.

Woe fell on matron and on maid,
  But Janet sped away,
High o'er the Scottish hills she hied
  To where the English lay.

She bade them lead her where their Chief
  Stood with his kinsmen near,
And though her heart beat fast the while,
  Her voice was calm and clear.

" I am a Fraser's lass, my Lord,
  Your grace I crave," she said,
Earl Widdington made answer thus,
  And bared his stately head :

" Your Chieftain's life is safe, my lass,
  His fetters I will break,
And let the men of Fraser's clan
  Go hence for your dear sake.

" You proved a steadfast friend to me
  When I was sore beset,
I loved you then with all my heart,
  I love you, lassie, yet.

" And here in presence of my kin,
  That all may understand,
I sue you for your plighted troth,
  I sue you for your hand."

" I crave your pardon if," said she,
  " I seem distraught in mind,

27

The eagles with the eagles mate,
    The thrushes seek their kind ;

" You have your hawks, you have your hounds,
    You have your bill and bow,
Such words will work me harm, my Lord,
    I prithee let me go."

His brother Hugh laughed loud and said,
" Now, by my troth, I swear
My haughty kin would doff the rose,
    And place the thistle there."

And while his kinsmen by his side
    Laughed loud with bitter scorn,
Lord Widdington, with flashing eyes,
    Leaned on his saddle-horn.

" I give thee escort, gentle maid,
    And home I go with thee ;
For, by Saint Ann, I will not brook
    These gibes and jeers," quoth he.

One blessed morn the wedding bells
    Pealed from the castle fane,
And he was Lord of Widdington,
    And she was Lady Jane.

HAR-MA-KHU.

THE SPHINX.

TO HOLD eternal vigil o'er the place,
By Ghiza's royal tomb it couchant lies
Beneath the solemn arch of Egypt's
skies,—
A nameless type of terror and of grace.

The toil and torment of a patient race,
Thou must have seen with fixed and stony eyes—
Have heard their hapless moans, their helpless
cries,
With that same tranquil and impassive face.

The seal of silence on thy lips is laid,
The myths are dumb, tradition gropes in vain
To solve the voiceless records of the dead;
And while the broken tablets fall and fade,
Defied by thee, the ages wax and wane,
And baffled Time goes by with noiseless tread.

❧

EL VAQUERO.

WINGED with the blood of Aztec lands,
Sphinx-like, the tawny herdsman stands,
A coiled reata in his hands.
Devoid of hope, devoid of fear,
Half brigand, and half cavalier,—
This helot, with imperial grace,
Wears ever on his tawny face
A sad, defiant look of pain.
Left by the fierce iconoclast,
A living fragment of the past,—
Greek of the Greeks he must remain.

29

DE PROFUNDUS.

THE waves were beating along the shore,
   And the wind swept by with a dismal
      moan,
As I entered the silent house once more,
   And groped my way to her room alone.

I had seen the pageant, and heard the prayer,
   And had watched the priest in the solemn rite,
But I could not think that my love lay there,
   Robed for the tomb in her garments of white.

And I sought her chamber with one sole thought,
   To find my love with her gentle face;
I could see the pictures her hand had wrought,
   And her bird still hung in its wonted place.

A knoted scarf, and the fillet which bound
   Her hair, lay there with its glittering pin;
I opened the leaves of a book, and found
   A rose I had given her pressed therein.

And I said she will surely come if I call,—
   She is only waiting to hear her name;
And I breathed the one she loved best of all,
   But the way was dark and she never came.

I was dazed and dumb, and my eyes were dry,
   And I watched and watched till the break of dawn,
Then the rain of my tears fell fast, and I
   Knew well that the life of my life was gone.

IN THE SIERRAS.

THE rocks loom o'er the tranquil vale,
　　Like ruins vast and hoary:
Each gray old turret has its tale,
　　Each seam and scar its story.

A hundred centuries have penned,
　　Upon these time-stained pages,
A secret lore, that is not kenned
　　By wisest seers and sages.

The fire, the frost, perchance the storms
　　Of some primeval ocean,
Have worn and torn the ragged forms,
　　This petrified commotion.

The years have softened all the scene,
　　The winds have sown the grasses;
And sun and rain have clothed with green,
　　The naked slopes and passes.

Here, on the granite crags I lie,
　　Lulled by the wind's low wailing
And watch against the distant sky,
　　The eagle slowly sailing.

The silver moon, with mellow ray,
　　Across yon spur is drifting;
The roseate tints of dying day
　　Along the west are shifting.

The gray mist gathers in the gorge,
　　Where bright cascades are flowing;
While like the gleam of lighted forge,
　　The snow-crowned peaks are glowing.

31

Rare pictures, born of sun and shade,
  Come with the evening shadows;
Night nestles in the silent glade,
  And veils the emerald meadows.

Above, the moaning pine trees stand;
  Below, the shining river;
Uncovered, in this temple grand,
  I worship God, the Giver.

♣

A MEMOGRAPH.

IT IS strange, as I look at the play to-night,
That her form and her features should flash
    on my sight.
The past and the present are set in the scene,
With the fathomless gulf of the years between;
While to and fro,
In the mimic show,
The ghosts of the actors come and go.
Time and the traces of time are gone,
And we live and move in the splendor of dawn.
As I saw her once, I can see her yet,
But her heart seems filled with a vague regret,
For when Juliet weeps, her cheeks are wet.
Who cares for the sneer of the wordly wise,
When youth looks down with its love-lit eyes.
Sir Romeo waits at the wings for his call,
And a strain of Strauss,
Thrills the breathless house,
While a glory and glamour are over it all.
O the sights, and the sounds, and the one face there,
With the rose I had given her twined in her hair.

TO THE UNKNOWN GOD.

ALL hail to Thee, Force of the Forces!
  The pulse of atomic vibration,
    The germ of conception and being,
      The impulse of matter and mind.
Thine, Thine, are the infinite sources,
  A function of endless duration,
    The rythm of sound and of seeing,
      The soul of the soul of mankind.

The myths of the centuries hoary,
  As told by the seers and the sages,
    Awaken a smile of derision
      At the faiths and the fables of yore.
We question the stars, and their story,
  Proclaimed by the audible ages,
    Reveals to our wondering vision
      The past and its mystical lore.

Thou, Thou art the motive and motion,
  The Life and the Life Everlasting,
    Which thrills and pervades and possesses
      Each atom in limitless space.
Men pay Thee a form of devotion,
  With sacrifice, penance, and fasting,
    To solace the soul that transgresses,
      For thus saith the Gospel of Grace.

Uncompassed of time and location,
  Fulfilled of desire and endeavor,
    The soul finds its final fruition,
      Dismantled of flesh and its thrall.
We pass from the stress of probation,
  To peace that endureth forever;
    For death is not death but transition;
      And Thou art the All and in All.

33

IN CALM AND STORM.

O SEA! thou art so false and yet so fair;
    Erewhile, in summer silence, thou didst
       sleep,
    And lazily, thy lapsing waves did creep
Along the shining sands, while here and there
A toying breath of soft autumnal air
   Dropped down to kiss and curl the drowsy deep.
So like a tigress lurking in her lair—
A serpent coiled to strike me unaware—
    For now thy marching waves in rythmic sweep,
    Like white-plumed squadrons, charge the scarped
      steep,
And reeling tempests rave and lightnings glare.
   O Sea! a ghastly harvest thou dost reap,
    While waiting wives and mothers watch and weep,
And yet thy lovers deem thee debonair.

❧

THE HUMMING-BIRD.

IN GOLD, and green, and purple sheen,
A winged meteor is seen.
With sharp, prismatic flash of light,
It shoots athwart the startled sight;
Plays on the lilac's purple bloom
With drone of wing and glint of plume;
Then on the calyx of the rose
An emerald gleams, a ruby glows;
A moment here, a moment there,
A moment poises in the air;
And then, across the open space,
The gem incarnate darts apace.

34

THE BUTTERFLY.

SEE, where the tortuous torrent glides,
Amid the leaves a pansy hides.
  I stoop to pluck it there,
    And lo, it swings,
    On living wings,
  Above me in the air.
Alas ! this oriental bloom
Is but the pretense of perfume ;—
A moth tricked out for masquerade,
In gold and purple robes arrayed.
A chrysalis would be a flower,
  And breaks its filmy thralls ;
Then on its flaunting wings it flies
    One little hour ;
    And when it dies,
  An oscillating spangle falls.

SUMMER DAYS.

HE CAME when stormy March was done,
  And April birds were on the wing,
When flush of sward and flash of sun
  Lent light and color to the spring.

His smile made glad the summer days,
  Until my foolish heart was stirred,
And as we walked the woodland ways,
  I listened to his whispered word.

Now fields with bloom are not besprent,
  And birds no longer pipe with glee ;
He took the summer when he went,
  And left the winter here to me.

35

HULDA.

I N A castle built of stone,
Hulda sits and sighs alone.

Since her ill-starred natal day,
Forty years have passed away.

Suitors had she by the score,
In the palmy days of yore.

Belted knights of high degree
Came to woo on bended knee.

High she held her stately head;
" I will wed a prince," she said.

Homeward rode the knights forlorn,
As she turned from them in scorn.

But the prince came nevermore,
In the palmy days of yore.

So she sits and sighs alone
In a castle built of stone.

❧

BEREFT.

A BIRD came down with the wind one morn,
   And nested in our tree;
That very day our babe was born,
   And then we numbered three.

But when the summer slipped away,
   Our roses turned to rue;
The bird took wing one autumn day,
   And we are only two.

ENGLAND AT BAY.

THEY have sought to revile you with jeers
and with laughter,
 Bold mother of empires, and mistress of
 seas;
Let them look to their bulwarks whenever, hereafter,
 The red cross of England is flung to the breeze.

From the Cape to the Baltic your pennants are flying;
 The Czar and the Kaiser may press their demands,
With a muster, ere long, of the dead and the dying,
 When the leash of the war hounds is slipped from
 your hands.

Do they think to dismay ? Do they dare to defy you ?
 Do they dream that the spirit of England is dead ?
It is well to recall, ere they seek to decry you,
 The fields where the blood of the Briton was shed.

If they read on the scroll of your grandeur and glory,
 The names that are deathless, the deeds that were
 done ;
They will learn how replete is the page of your story,
 How great are the triumphs which freedom has
 won,

In the hush of the tempest your foes are creating ;
 Ere the tocsin is sounded, the banners unfurled,
We can see on the ramparts, the Lion in waiting,
 Alone and undaunted, confronting the world.

37

THE DEATH-WATCH.

O YOUR measure of bliss was more than
  filled
  When you drank the wine of her lips;
You reeled with delight while your pulses
  thrilled
To the touch of her finger tips.

Her form is so fine and her face so fair,
  And her voice so low when she speaks;
The hue of the primrose is on her hair,
  And the tint of dawn on her cheeks.

God gave her the face of a saint, and you
  Saw her only in saintly guise;
'Tis barely a month since she vowed to be true,
  This woman with wonderful eyes.

'Tis barely a month, but her vows are vain,
  And she meets you with cool repose;
Not a pulse of passion or pang of pain
  Do her wonderful eyes disclose.

Your hope is a corpse, and with pallid brow
  You stand by the pall of the dead;
Only the death-watch is left you now;
  So watch there with eyelids of lead.

FOUR SCORE YEARS AND TEN.

FROM that far distant goal, he seems to cast
His patient eyes across the vanished
years;
Life's turmoil, with its triumphs and its
tears,
Is now a part of that relentless past.
The eager feet, which erstwhile sped so fast,
Urged ever onward by his hopes and fears,
Have reached the utmost verge of life at last,
Where that grim warder of the grave appears.
Firm in the faith that all is for the best,
Like some spent toiler he would take his rest.
For good or ill his little work is done;
Far from the silver radiance of the dawn,
The fervid heat and flame of noon are gone;
He only waits the setting of the sun.

❦

THE HUNGRY HEART.

ABOU HAIRI—world renowned—
Tells how a starving Arab found
A diamond lying on the ground.

" Oh, if this shining stone, instead,
Were but a single date," he said,
" A cruse of oil, a crust of bread."

The rarest jewels of the mine
Upon the heaving breast may shine,
And yet the hungry heart will pine.

39

For the wind is a trifle fresh to-day,
And who knows, poor things, but a taste of salt spray
  Might change all their sorrow to joy."

In less than an hour, with eight or ten more,
  We had them on board of our staunch little craft;
The sails were all set, we standing off shore,
While the spray from the white-caps were flying
    before,
  And the wind followed hard abaft.

Just how it all happened, we never could tell;
  The child leaned on the rail by her grandpapa's
  side ;
Our weather-bow must have been caught by the
  swell,
For there came a lurch, and a cry, and she fell —
  And something white floated off on the tide.

Tom held the helm ; in an instant he swung
  And brought her to in the eye of the gale ;
Two men were over, one old and one young.
  But young arms are lusty, not likely to fail—
  And how does my blithe, bonny bird like the tale ?

What ! You wish to hear more of the old emigre ?
  Not satisfied yet ?—it seems incomplete ?
Well, look in my eyes. Don't you see, chere amie,
I—I was the lad who leaped into the sea,
  And you—you were " ma pauvre petite."

42

MY ORIENT.

SPELL-BOUND beside the languid stream,
   Breathing the lotus balm,
I lie amid the ferns and dream
   Of Oriental palms.

Where now, with most ungainly strides,
   The lazy heron feeds,
Methinks the sacred ibis hides
   Among the river reeds.

The sunbeam's golden arrows fall
   About me in the grass ;
I hear the midges' bugle-call
   To combat, as they pass.

I see the emmets' pyramid,
   And watch their caravans,
Like camels on the march amid
   Sahara's desert sands.

One horseman dashes o'er the plain,
   One stands beside the gate ;
Al Hassan seeks the camel train,
   While Mahmoud lies in wait.

An aged sheik, with wrinkled brows,
   Sits in the evening sun,
And gathers dates from oaken boughs,
   As I perhaps have done.

The silent twilight hour draws near,
   The crescent gleams in air,
And I expectant, wait to hear
   Muezzin's call to prayer.

ART ETERNAL.

WHAT marvels, wrought in tint and tone,
  The Master's fruitful hand hath told
On frescoed nave and carven stone:
  Where " Hail the Victor " rang of old,
When proud triumphal chariots rolled
Along the far-famed Appian way;
  How Cæsar's gauds are bought and sold,
While Art, eternal, holds its sway.

The world a stage, from zone to zone,
  The mimic kings and queens have strolled,
With laugh and jest, and sigh and moan:
  Their words of fire are fierce and bold,
  Their words of scorn are calm and cold,
Or light or tender, sad or gay,
  They turn their tinsel into gold,
While Art, eternal, holds its sway.

Strange airs, from Delphian slopes, are blown,
  Since erst the wing-ed horse was foaled;
Across the years the spell is thrown,
  And fast within our hearts we hold
  A wealth no miser's hand hath doled:
The king, by grace of God to-day,
  May die, and lie beneath the mould,
While Art, eternal, holds its sway.

ENVOY.

O fair-haired Goddess! silver stoled,
  We dance in dreams, with Faun and Fay,
And pipe with Pan adown the wold,
  While Art, eternal, holds its sway.

44

WHO KNOWS?

CONFRONTED from within and from without,
   By vague, uncertain questions that arise;
Condemned if only we presume to doubt
The dogmatists whom mortals canonize.

Must we without complaint, deceived, undone,
   Cold-eyed and calm, accept the cruel fate,
Which robs us of our treasures one by one,
   And still unsated leaves us desolate?

Must we conceal our motives from the world,
   And sacrifice our candor to our fears?
And while the heart is crushed must lips be curled,—
   A frozen sneer above a sea of tears?

Must face and voice—by subtle sense or sight,
   Which we have somewhere seen or heard before—
With strange perverseness haunt us day and night,
   The fabled skeleton behind the door?

Prometheus-like, must we with hopeless sighs,
   Chained and dejected, pace the weary round,
Seeking with hungered hearts and eager eyes,
   The something longed for, and yet never found?

Will no fruition come with calm repose,
   When death rings down the curtain to the play?
By his harmonious law and love—who knows?—
   Perchance the problem may be solved some day.

THE DERELICT.

UNMOORED, unmanned, unheeded on the
   deep—
   Tossed by the restless billow and the
     breeze,
It drifts o'er sultry leagues of tropic seas,
Where long Pacific surges swell and sweep.
When pale-faced stars their silent watches keep,
  From their far rythmic spheres, the Pleiades,
  In calm beatitude, and tranquil ease,
Smile sweetly down upon its cradled sleep.
Erewhile, with anchor housed, and sails unfurled,
  We saw the stout ship breast the open main,
To round the Stormy Cape, and span the world,
  In search of ventures which betoken gain.
To-day, somewhere, on some far sea, we know
Her battered hulk is heaving to and fro.

❧

PREMONITION.

I QUESTIONED my soul as I stood by the
   dead,
   My soul in its anguish, made answer and
     said,
No power can destroy, and no fiat create,
For death is transition, and life is a state,
The fruit of conditions coercive as fate.
Each atom of form, and each atom of force
Exist as a part of their infinite source;
And whether in motion, or whether at rest,
Must live, by a law that is never transgressed.
This then is the marvelous secret of death,
To live without life, and to breathe without breath.

46

THE GLOAMING.

HE West is in a blaze of gold ;
  The day in regal splendor dies,
And silence falls on field and fold.

While, in the East, I now behold
  The full-faced moon in glory rise,
The West is in a blaze of gold.

The darkness deepens in the wold,
  And soft the evening zephyr sighs,
And silence falls on field and fold.

As timid stars, grown overbold,
  Peep, one by one, from out the skies,
The West is in a blaze of gold.

The gowan nestles in the mould,
  The dewdrop on the heather lies,
And silence falls on field and fold.

The hearth is warm, the heath is cold,
  A wight, belated, homeward hies,
The West in a blaze of gold,
And silence falls on field and fold.

CON AMORE—CON DOLORE.

1872.   1896.

I MIND me of that long-gone year,
When stout Jo Tilden planned the cheer,
   And Chismore wrote the clever verses ;
We sat and hatched our quibbles queer,
And Parker brought us pots of beer,
   If we had shekels in our purses.

I see them in the waning lights,
The frantic Barbour in his tights,
   And Beard, the grangers' friend and brother ;
And Hawes who made such valiant fights,
On voting days and tilting nights,
   Just now coquetting with another.

And Clay and Caspar, Jack and John,
And Frank and Ned, and Will and Juan,
   And genial Clint, the would-be punster ;
And George, but more of him anon,
The Count, the Baron, and the Don,
   And Royal Dan the King of Munster.

Still Doctor Behr's rare wit I hear,
See Tommy Newcomb's smiling sneer,
   And bold Smith Clark and Major Bender ;
Cremony's grim, sardonic leer,
Half brigand and half cavalier,
   And yet his heart was soft and tender.

We have our lares in the hall,
Our pictured Saints upon the wall,
   Our outward comforts and our inner ;
There's John and Peter, James and Paul,

48

And Jo who is no Saint at all,
  But such a cool, delightful sinner.

A would-be monk in gabardine,
Charles Warren is his name I ween,
  His " South Sea Idyls " has forsaken ;
And dear Prince Hal with courtly mien,
A pair of demoiselles between,
  Is overmatched, or I'm mistaken.

There's Captain Jim, we call him pere.
As stanch and true as Legadare,
  For words of praise he would not thank me ;
Our shelves speak louder than I dare,
I hope with him one day to share,
  That heaven where he will outrank me.

Lo, Uncle George with face benign,
As mellow as Falernian wine,
  And sparkling as the widow Cliquot ;
Long may we hear that voice of thine,
As in the days of auld lang syne,
  Long life to thee my old amigo.

Ho youngsters, cease your rant and roar,
The roll is being called once more,
  We mark the missing con dolore ;
The dead outcount us by a score,
The best perhaps have gone before,
  " Lord love us " was our toast of yore,
And thus we pledge you, con amore.

PADRE KINO.

AS READ in old monastic lore,
　　So runs the legend of traditions,
　Two hundred years ago and more,
　Along Pimeria's arid shore,
　　Were seen a hundred white-walled missions.

Throughout the drear and desert lands,
　Where roamed fierce tribes intent on pillage,
From Blanca's snows to Gila's sands,
Transformed by consecrated hands,
　Bloomed fertile fields with careful tillage.

And where the iridescent morn
　Once lit the waste with tinted lustres,
Amalthea filled her fabled horn
From meadows rank with tasseled corn,
　And hillsides flushed with purple clusters.

The subtle skill which deftly tilled
　The barren dunes and sterile places,
By power assumed and pledge fulfilled,
And timely word and deed, instilled
　In savage breasts the Christian graces.

The mission bells betimes invite
　To prayer and praise and prompt confession ;
With awe the humble neophyte,
On bended knees, each morn and night,
　Tells o'er his beads in deep contrition.

No Cortez, with his lances keen,
　On conquest bent has hither drifted ;
Only a sandled monk is seen,
With patient grace and prudent mien,
　And sacred symbol high uplifted.

50

Inspired to found a new crusade,
  With fervent faith and fixed devotion,
From Salamanca's cloistered shade,
In mail of righteousness arrayed,
  The Padre Kino crossed the ocean.

Within that sanctified retreat,
  Absorbed in holy meditations,
While kneeling at Immanuel's feet,
He heard the voice divine repeat,
  "Go preach my gospel to all nations."

The sainted hero's race is run ;
  We read with tears the touching story,
Of how, by daily penance done,
And Christian faith and works, he won
  At last the martyr's crown of glory.

The years, with their remorseless hands,
  Have ground to dust the white-walled missions;
And, in the place of fruitful lands,
Have left us but the drifting sands,
  The broken shrines, the old traditions.

.

THE ICEBERG.

LO ! ON our weather bow there seems to be
   A spectral ship which gives no answering
     hail ;
   Its stealthy presence makes the stoutest
     quail,
And as we reach to windward fast and free,
We leave the floating phantom on our lee,
   To drift from zone to zone without avail,
   The toy of tossing tide and driving gale—
A white-robed spectre on the wide, wide sea.
   High O'er the frozen bulwark flies the spray,
And through the mist a shaft of sunlight streams ;
   Amid the ghostly shrouds the rainbows play,
And all the frosted fretwork glints and gleams—
   Drift on to be dissolved, and then to rise,
   Type of the soul that dies, and never dies.

❦

THE ROSE AND THE THORN.

A YOUTH, once walking in the early dawn,
Espied a red rose blushing on the lawn.

Its simple beauty caught his fickle sight,
Its subtile perfume filled him with delight.

With eager, selfish haste, that self-same morn,
He plucked the rose, unmindful of the thorn.

Alas, alack-a-day ! his joy has fled :
Only the thorn remains ; the rose is dead.

52

SUTTER'S FORT.

I STOOD by the old fort's crumbling wall,
  On the eastern verge of the town ;
The sun through cliffs in the ruined hall,
  Flecked with its light the rafters brown.

And, sifting with gold the oaken floor,
  Seemed to burnish the place anew ;
While out and in, through the half-closed door,
  Building their nests, the swallows flew.

Charmed by the magic spell of the place,
  The present vanished, the past returned ;
While rampart and fortress filled the space,
  And yonder the Indian camp-fires burned.

I heard the sentinel's measured tread,
  The challenge prompt, the quick reply ;
I saw on the tower, above my head,
  The Mexican banner flaunt the sky.

Around me were waifs from every clime,
  Blown by the fickle winds of chance ;
Knights-errant, ready at any time,
  For any cause, to couch a lance.

The stanch old captain, with courtly grace,
  Owner of countless leagues of land,
Benignly governs the motly race,
  Dispensing favors with open hand.

His long-horned herds on the wild oats feed,
  While brown vaqueros, with careless rein,
Swinging reatas, at headlong speed
  Are dashing madly over the plain.

53

Only a moment the vision came ;
 Where tower and rampart stood before,
Where flushed the night with the camp's red
  flame,
 Dust and ashes and nothing more.

Borne to my ear on the ambient air,
 Mingled with sounds of childish glee,
I heard again the low hum of care,
 Like the restless moan of the sea.

❧

EL SALVADORE.

A CRESCENT bay, and crested peaks on
  high,
 With wooded flanks, which seaward
  slope between,
 Embossed with fold on fold of deathless green,
And over all an arch of turquoise sky.

Thus I recall with half-regretful sigh,
 The sights and sounds of that exotic scene ;—
 Its wealth of tint and tone, its airs serene,
Which erstwhile charmed my wistful ear and eye.

A dreamy land of indolence and ease,—
With budding boughs and vines, and fruited trees,
 Where birds on gold and scarlet wings flash by :
Beside a reed-thatched hut nude children play,
While to and fro the palm trees idly sway,
 And spent waves swoon upon the shore and die.

AN OFT TOLD TALE.

I RECOLLECT one certain night in June,
  (It seems to me our nights are dearer
      than our days,)
  When dust of silver from the moon,
  (As some familiar poet says,)
Fell softly on the sea and land.
  It was the night of nights ; pray tell what harm
  For youth and beauty, arm in arm,
To saunter down the yellow sand?
  I quite forget just how it came about ;
  There was an earnest word, two hands held out,
And then upon his breast,
In momentary rest,
  The mobile mouth and tender eyes
  Were turned to him in glad surprise.
It was so very, very nice you know,
  To press her seaside hat against his vest,
A sweet foretaste of heaven, although
  The rest was only momentary rest ;
For with remorseful start she said,
  " Alas ! Alas ! for me,
  It cannot, cannot be,
To-morrow week I am to wed."
  How small a word will grind the heart to dust ;
A breath of air will break the thread
  On which we hang our trust ;
And while his lips were white and mute,
He took from her the Dead Sea fruit,
  And simply bowed his head.
An oft told tale ; it was the wealth
Of youth and hope, and matchless health ;
  It was the opulence of brawny arms

55

Against the rent roll of a hundred farms.
Back to his dull, unconscious books
    He went, with bruis-ed heart and sharpened brain,
To school his thoughts, and mask his looks,
    And nurse a purpose born of pain.
A trifle cynical he seems, and yet
He may, perhaps, forget.
    "Hard hit," Sir Blase says in well bred slang;
    He sees the symptoms and has felt the pang.
Brave hearts will sometimes wince, he knows;
    Will wince, and still not whine,
If once there is no color to the rose,
    No sparkle to the wine.
And she, she plays her wedded part
Right royally, with subtle art;
    And wears with pride her gilded chain;
But for the semblance of a heart
        We seek in vain.
    The man whose name she bears
    Is old and grey and bent with cares;
        But then, but then,
        He is the prince of men,
For she is mistress of the Riverside,
And has a brown stone front in town beside.
    Time brings reprisals to us all,
And soon or late we learn the truth,
    That stately pride will have its fall;
And that one little heart, forsooth,
        Outweighs it all.

THE MUSE OF ROMANCE.

YOU are known, I believe, as a man about
town,
If you go as you ought to the Bas Bleu
soiree,
You will meet Mrs. D. in a chic Paris gown;
She will chat, as she toys with her fan and bouquet,
Of the lyrics, and lays of Mistral and Daudet,
And will even repeat, sub rosa, perchance,
The refrain of Gringoire with an accent Anglais,
For the fad of the hour is the Muse of Romance.

You will doubtless encounter a stare and a frown
From a prig who pretends to be wise and au fait;
For the "Set" will insist you should know Mr.
Brown,
But the Lord knows who Brown is, I don't, nor
do they;—
Though his father made his money in "Ophir,"
they say;
He's Sir Oracle now, you will see at a glance,
And has written a double ballade, by the way,
For the fad of the hour is the Muse of Romance.

As for me, give me rather the heath and the down,
The glory of Autumn, the freshness of May,
The bold mountain peak with its white-crested
crown,
The hiss of the squall, and the flash of the spray;—
A fig for the fustian of frill and of fray,
The knight and the lady, the tilt and the dance,
The gay cavalcade and the stately array,
Though the fad of the hour is the Muse of Romance.

57

ENVOY.

Ho Villon ! you conjured the rhymes of your day,
  Like a bold troubadour and a gallant free-lance,
But your ghost is disturbed, and the devil's to pay,
  For the fad of the hour is the Muse of Romance.

❧

THEN AND NOW.

A VAULTED roof, a columned nave,
  An oriel window whence the light
Gilds fretted arch and architrave,
  As moonlight gilds the night.
The old, old story of the heart ;
  Beside the chancel, hand in hand,
A ring, a vow " till death do part,"
  Two wedded lovers stand.

A cold, dark sky, a darker sea,
  A foaming fringe of breaking surf ;
Beside a gnarled and leafless tree,
  A patch of tender turf.
A woman kneeling on the sands,
  Two white lips parted as in prayer,
A Niobe with outstretched hands,
  Wrestling with fell despair.

AN ALLEGORY.

SWEET Floribel,
I fain would tell
What once befell
Our neighbor's starling, on a time :
  Fed by a tender hand, it hung
  Upon a gilded perch, and sung,
    Until, alas ! one hapless day,
  Lured by a bird-note from the lime,
    In wantonness it flew away.

Somewhere the fowler's snare is spread ;
  Unwary feet are sure to trip ;
Forbidden fruits are sweet, 'tis said,
  Yet turn to ashes on the lip.

Some fleeting, evanescent hours—
Amid the birds, amid the flowers—
  Two silken wings were plumed with pride ;
Then came the bitter night,
And ere the morning light
  Our birdling drooped and died.

WHAT MATTERS IT WHERE OR WHEN?

An Episode of The Morgue.

I AM tired of the bicker and banter of life,
    I am tired of serfdom and thrall,
I am tired of the stress and the strain and
    the strife,
    I am tired of it all.

  •   •   •   •   •   •   •   •   •

The ghost of my comrades come back to-night
    When the battle is well-nigh done ;
How many there were who went down in the fight,
    And how few there were who won.

I put my head down on my hands and think
    Of the hopes that have passed me by,
Of the woman who gave me a cup to drink,
    And left me to drain it dry.

I am worn and weary, and long for rest,
    And there's no one to watch and weep ;
This life is only an hour at its best,
    And after—a dreamless sleep.

The grim scythe-bearer so gaunt and thin,
    Reaps ever his harvest of men ;
And sooner or later will garner us in,
    What matters it where or when ?

So here's to the fellow who laughs at fate,
    And falls with his face to the foe ;
The embers are dead in the blackened grate—
    I bid you good-night, and go.

DRIFTING.

CROSS San Pablo's heaving breast
   I see the home-lights gleam,
As the sable garments of the night
   Drop down on vale and stream.

The daylight on his royal couch
   In crimson glory dies,
While northward on belated wing,
   The sad-voiced bittern flies.

For miles—from where yon rounded hills
   Darken the southern sky—
I hear the bells of browsing kine,
   And catch the herder's cry.

Just where the silver of the moon
   Falls on the shimmering tide,
Marking that line of light, I see
   Twin islands side by side.

Hard by, yon vessel from the seas
   Her cargo homeward brings,
And soon, like sea-bird on her nest,
   Will sleep with folded wings.

The fisher's boat swings in the bay,
   From yonder point below,
While ours is drifting with the tide,
   And rocking to and fro ;

Carelessly rocking to and fro,
   As shifts the fitful stream ;
Two Nimrods dreaming as we drift,
   And sketching as we dream.

"TINS TO MEND!"

"TINS to mend!" How he swings along,
That curious man with his tattered clothes,
And his swarthy face, and his crooked nose,
And that nasal chant wherever he goes,
  Quaint burlesque of a song.

The vagrant life he leads, who knows?
Through the highways and byways, out and in
Searching early and late for worn-out tin;
The housemaid declares that he smells of gin—
  He don't seem like a rose.

As I watched him that autumn day,
I marveled if perchance some biting scorn,
Or a blighted hope, or a life forlorn,
Had not changed the gold of his early morn
  Into an ashen gray.

And where fell first his childhood's glance—
Whether by Vineland's hilled and castled stream,
Or where the Bosphor's storied waters gleam,
Or Adriatic's thousand islands seem
  The haunts of old romance.

" Tins to mend! " was the weird refrain
Which fell on my ear as I strolled along,
Farther and farther from the city's throng,
Till by an humble cot he ceased his song,
  From toil set free again.

The door ajar, I saw him kissed;
A little child, with sweet, endearing cry,
Sprang to his arms, love beaming from her eye;
Mine own were somehow wet—I can't tell why—
  It might have been the mist.

62

The good God keeps us in His sight—
Sure, if in pleasant paths our footsteps fall,
Or if our dead hopes lie beneath the pall,
That joy and sorrow come alike to all,
    That morn succeeds the night.

❧

TO HENRY IRVING.

Read at a dinner given to Mr. Irving by the Bohemian Club,
San Francisco, September 10, 1893.

IN THIS our realm, heart speaks to heart;
        and here
    Upon the utmost verge of western lands,
    With honest Saxon speech and cordial
        hands,
We give you greeting hearty and sincere.
    You touch the zenith in your wondrous role:
We hear again the voice of that grand age
    When Avon's Bard unmasked the very soul,
And left its secrets on his deathless page.
    No narrow ties entrammel us, but we
Hail him as Master who takes foremost part
In the wide world of letters and of art.
    To that historic land beyond the sea,
Where hawthorn hedges bloom and daisies blow,
Our hearts and hopes go with you when you go.

A MONOGRAPH.

ANNO DOMINI eighteen thirty-one,
In the third year of wedlock, there was born,
To John and Josephine, an only son.
Thus much was written on his birth-day
morn.
Swarthed, nursed, and christened, as befits the heir
Of honest yeomen, he waxed stout and fair :
Until at length, well grown, he quit the fold.
A few strong headlines, and the rest is told.
 A mother's hopes, a mother's fears,
 A school-boy's triumphs and his tears,
 A dear girl's love, a stolen kiss,
 A mutual vow, for good or ill,
 A year or more of wedded bliss,
 A new-made grave beyond the hill.
 The bitter pang, the life-long pain,
 The transient pleasures of an hour,
 The shifting tides of loss and gain,
 The bootless strife for place and power.
 He joined the ranks where brave men fell,
 He saw the battle's lurid glare,
 He heard the scream of shot and shell,
 The rolling drums, the trumpets blare.
 Amid the windrows of the dead
 I knelt to-day beside his bed.
 He died as men have died before,
 A spent wave on a barren shore.
 We storm the fortress, and we fail ;
 We dream of eagle-flights, and fall.
 I have writ down an o'er-true tale ;
 Alas ! God help us,—that is all.

NEITHER DO I CONDEMN.

I'VE sent for you, Will. I know you won't
    mind;
  You were always so silent and good—
When others were rude and unkind,
  You alone understood.

Please bring your chair here, Will, close to my side.
  There—lift my head. I've something to say.
Oh, I thought last night I'd have died;
  How I longed for the day.

Well again soon—do you think? Alas! no.
  This pain at my heart like a knife—
But it matters not when I go
  Out of this weary life.

Now, promise me, Will, to do what I ask;
  And bend down while I whisper my name;
For women like me wear a mask
  To cover and hide their shame.

There's a little brown house on the hillside,
  And a white-haired old man left alone—
Oh, Will, if you knew how I've tried
  All these years to atone.

Here's a package, a letter, and something more;
  A lock of my hair—don't think it a whim;
Send them, dear Will, when all is o'er,
  With a kind word to him.

Conceal from him all of my wickednesses;
  Say that my heart ran over with love—

65

That I died, praying God to bless
    And unite us above.

Perhaps the dear God will forgive the sin
    For the sake of His Son crucified,
And permit me to enter in,
    Pardoned and purified.

Back of the town—on the slope, to the west—
    Is a little grave; What! tears in your eyes?
Lay me there by her side to rest—
    There where my baby lies.

O God! This pain—it is coming. Hark!
    I shall die—don't leave me. Stay, Will, stay!
I'm going—your promise—so dark—
    Pray for me, Will, oh, pray!

Dead. Let not the living adjudge the dead;—
    Unworthy to touch His garment's hem;
Remember the Master hath said,
    " Neither do I condemn."

EL RIO SACRAMENTO.

WHERE ice-clad summits greet the morn,
And where the beetling crags look down
On dark blue lakes with sullen frown,
This bantling of the clouds is born.
Forth from its granite cradle creeps,
At first in play it laughs and leaps,
And then in dusky pools it sleeps.
Down silent sunless glens it glides,
And under long sedge grasses hides,
Where aspen leaves, like quivering wings,
Quaver above its hidden springs.

Anon, in silver-sheeted falls,
It leaps the terraced mountain walls,
And tumbles into rocky urns,
Beflecked with foam and fringed with ferns.
At last this half-grown infant, fed
By melting snow and falling rain,
Like Bruin chafing with his chain,
Growls hoarsely in its granite bed,
And ploughs its pathway to the plain.
Meanwhile, by some designing will
Harnessed and schooled, it turns the mill,
And with its ponderous sledge unlocks
The concrete coffers of the rocks.

In middle summer, lank and lean,
It creeps the shelving banks between;
And then in spring and autumn tide,
Crimson with carnage, flushed with pride,
In serried ranks of gleaning peaks
It dashes on the yielding dikes,

67

And breaks the ramparts, rushing down
Upon defenseless farm and town.

In tamer moods content to hold
By croft and thorp, by field and fold,
Past orchard boughs and bending grain,
Past grazing herds and loaded wain,
Past children laughing at their play,
The devious tenor of its way.

In ceaseless, silent sweep, between
Low-lying meadows, rank and green,
Along the marge of bastioned banks,
Its dimpled face reflect the ranks
Of gray-beard oaks; its liquid kiss
Thrills all the river reeds with bliss;
The thirsty fibrils of the vine
Reach down to quaff its amber wine;
The grasses and the willows lave
Their tangled tresses in its wave.
The silver thread has grown to be
A molten avalanche set free.
Its path the highway of the world,
Where sails of commerce are unfurled.
Emblem of Time's resistless tide,
On, and still on, its currents glide,
Until, at length, far, far below,
It weds the sea, with stately flow.

THE MESSIAH.

HIS was the coming which the seers foresaw,
His was the glory which men long to see,
He was the God who died for you and me,
And we accept the sacrifice with awe.

His life and teachings are to us divine,
They furnish dole for every human need;
We would discard no dogma of the creed,
Nor blot a word, nor abrogate a line.

No doubting thought can turn our gold to dross,—
No sceptic sneer can hang our heaven with gloom;
And so we weep with Mary at the cross,
And humbly kneel with Mary at the tomb.
The banner of our Lord is now unfurled,—
The dead Christ lives and dominates the world.

VICTORIA.

REGINA IMPERATRIX.

Read at the Jubilee Banquet, San Francisco, June 21, 1897.

O WOMAN whose annals can never be torn
From the record of England's renown;
How wisely and well in your day you have
borne
The burdens of scepter and crown.
Your hand on the pulse of the people, you feel
The throb that responds to your own;
Their will is the will, and their weal is the weal
Of the Commons, the Lords, and the Throne.

Evolved by the fates and adjusted by time,
The poise of the nation is true;
Its future is fixed and its past is sublime,
And its glory is symboled in you.
Not the prowess of England, the might of her arms,
Wherever her flag is unfurled;
But the clang of her hammers, the tilth of her farms,
Have won her the marts of the world.

Your reign has been marked by the triumphs of peace,
Resplendent in letters and art;
O that war and the rumors of war may cease,
Is the cry of your woman's heart.
Type of all that is noblest in mother and wife,
We hail you, O Empress and Queen!
God save you! and grant that your autumn of life
Be peaceful, benign and serene.

TO J. D. R.

AU REVOIR.

BOON comrade, in a hundred brilliant bouts,
Where wit with wit played carte and
tierce full fast,
With eager thrust and parry to the last,
We've hailed thee victor knight with pealing shouts.

And in life's ups and downs and ins and outs,
When weaklings wait and folly stands aghast,
Fail not, Sir Knight, to prick, as in the past,
The thin pretense of shams, the fears of doubts.

'Tis well betimes, in our prosaic land,
To conjure up the days of old romance,
When simple faith was more than sordid might.
And if so be the hour and age demand,
We look to see thee, armed with sword and lance,
Go forth to strike for God and for the right.

71

TENT-LIFE

TENT-LIFE.

AN HOUR of toil and strife, and we are dead.
Life is a lie, a bitter lie, I said,
And death itself is only dust to dust.
All men are mad indeed with venal lust,
The toiling gally slaves of cent per cent,
There is no cure, alas! for all these ills.
In such a mood I folded up my tent
In sooth, and sought the freedom of the hills.
And from the couch of pine-boughs where I lie,
I watch the miracle of dawning day :
And as the sable curtain rolls away,
And one by one, the dark winged shadows fly,
The earth, awaking from the cool embrace
Of night, reveals to me her rosy face.
Although the impress of repose remains,
The seal of sleep is broken ; to the ear
Come palpitating waves of sound ; I hear
The life-tide ebb and flow in nature's veins.
Tones inarticulate, the stir of wings,
The mellow murmur of earth's viewless springs.
And when Aurora's banners flaunt the skies,
And full-orbed day in regal pomp is born ;
I shake the spell of slumber from my eyes,
And hie me forth elate to meet the morn.

Come forth, O weary denizen of town,
Bathe in the sunshine, breathe the balmy air,
Shake off the toils of traffic, and lay down
The life-long burden which you seem to bear.
Wait not for death to break thy prison bars,
And send thy ransomed soul to paradise ;
But seek betimes, the free glad life beneath the stars.

75

For thee the gods have spread a rich repast ;
Ambrosia falls like manna from the skies,
  And nectar flows in every wayside rill.

Come forth, and break, for once, thy life-long fast,
  And from this gracious bounty take thy fill.
With eager step I climb the ridge to seek
A highland glade beneath the purple peak.
  There all the shining day, from dawn till dark,
The wary birds beneath the covert hide.
  Meanwhile my dogs exalt with bound and bark,
And beat the tangled brake from side to side.
  Borne onward by the day's advancing light,
  The waves of warmth roll down the rocky height,
And long before the ardent sun has kissed
  The humid lowlands with his earliest beam,
  I catch the gleam and sparkle of the stream,
Between the fading folds of silver mist.
  From nook and nest, when full-fledged day is born,
  What swarms of life comes forth to greet the morn.

  The drowsy hum of the bee is heard,
    And the locust's clanging cry ;
  And a flashing gem in the form of a bird,
    On its jeweled wings darts by.
  The linnet sings in the lowly hedge,
    And the raven croaks above ;
  The lizard basks on the crannied ledge,
    And the hawk swoops down on the dove.
  The dragon-fly like a fiend is seen,
    Poised in mid-air on his gauze-like wings ;
  And beetles, and moths in gold and green,
    And wasps with their shining rings.
  Spiders are weaving their filmy snares,
  76

And bees are hoarding their honeyed stores,
While emmets, busy with household cares,
  Trail over the forest floors.
Butterflies creep from the silken pall
  In the tomb where the chrysalis dies.
And through brooding leaves the sunbeams fall,
  And luminous columns of light arise.
In these shafts of light, from morn to night,
The midges reel in their amorous flight.
  The marmots chatter, the magpies scold,
And quails are piping along the slopes;
  And, down in the heart of the dusky wold,
The owl sits alone in his crypt, and mopes.
  Through the reedy marsh the bitterns wade,
And along the marge the herons stalk;
  The rabbit scurries across the glade,
And over the canon wheels the hawk.

I skirt along the mountain's bosky flank,
And find primeval parks of pines and firs.
Between the shoulders of projecting spurs,
  These lordly cones are marshaled rank on rank.
In the ambrosial gloom, dark aisles of pines
  Lead out to sunny glades, and laughing water-ways,
  Where moss-enameled trunks and trailing vines
Hedge in the bud and bloom of vernal days.
  Down the cool distance of the long arcade,
The white azalea's snow-flakes fleck the way;
  And in the shelter of the fostering shade,
I pluck one hooded violet of May.
  The fragrance of the flower-embroidered mead
Fills all the dreamy air with fresh delight.
Undaunted, from some far sequestered height,

The doe leads here her spotted fawns to feed;
And here the bee and bird and butterfly
Find spread for them a floral feast on high.
　Borne on tides of air, now faint, now clear,
　The roar of waters break upon my ear.
A shower of brook-notes floods the perfect day,
　Where sun-rays pierce the meshes of the mist,
An arch of splendor spans the falling spray.
　Haply some Naiad haunts the stream; I list
The sibylistic whisper of the leaves;
A Faun seems grieving when the fir-tree grieves,
　And in the pine's pathetic monotone
　Methinks I hear the sad-voiced Ariel moan.
Drenched by the rain of ceaseless waterfalls,
Moist-footed mosses scale the dripping walls.
　Here, wary of the angler's tempting hook,
　The lithe and spotted leopard of the brook
　Lurks for his prey in every shaded nook.
With ruffled crest, and sharp, discordant cries,
　The feathered fisher flits from limb to limb.
Into the fret and foam the ouzel flies,
　Above the nether pool the swallows skim.
This is the gate-way—and on either hand
　The fragments of colossal cliffs. I climb
From rock to rock, until at last I stand
　Upon the ragged battlements of time.
The earth's historian is death; and here,
　From age to age, are stamped the records of the
　　past.
Man and his handiwork may disappear,
　But these shall last as long as time shall last.
In the archaic years, the glacier's fangs
　Laid bare these granite ribs, and ground to dust

78

The concrete layers of the lava crust.
Rents, riven by the earthquake, mark the pangs
  Of nature, and reveal to us the throes
Of earth. These rounded domes, these cloudcap spires,
  Congealed and moulded into grand repose,
Bespeak the fury of volcanic fires.
  Down the long pathway of the ages, time
Has wrought with magic touch, transmuting all
  The fearful splendors of creation's prime.
And as the æons rolled away, the pall
  Was lifted from the sea and land, and life
  Was born of death, the elemental strife
Was hushed, the Voice Divine was heard, peace
    reigned,
And beauty blossomed in the earth.   Ordained
  By some fixed law, the seasons come and go.
The wind-sown seeds in desert places sleep,
  Until the sunbeams kiss the dust, when lo !
The hidden germs are stirred, the heavens weep,
  And life triumphant springs from last year's tomb.
Into the crannied rock and lichens creep,
  Along the crater's rim the roses bloom.
The streams, from winter's icy chain set free,
  And fed by falling rain and melting snow,
  Rush down the ice-worn water-ways and flow
In melted music to the summer sea.
  Within the mountain's lap enshrined,
And where the falling waters wake
  A thousand echoes from the cliffs, I find
A rock imprisoned lake.
  Locked in a glacier's tomb, it lies asleep,
Belted by firs, and fringed with water-plants.
Upon its shining disk the sunbeams dance,

79

And from its polished lips the rapids leap.
Seen through the water's cool eclipse, behold,
  Suspended in its calm, unruffled breast,
The hanging outlines of the dusky wold,
  And the inverted headlands of the crest.
Lured by the wild seclusion of the place,
Its savage grandeur and its tender grace ;
  Lulled by the ripple of the wind and tide,
  The incense, and the song of birds, I bide
A blissful moment ; and as I depart
  I turn from thee, O tranquil lake, and hide
A picture and a poem in my heart.
Three hours, at least, since dawn, and here we are ;—
  Ten miles, o'er mount and moor, as flies the crow,
  The skulking covey now is near at hand,
My dogs have snuffed the battle from afar ;
  How quick they catch the scent, how stanch they
      stand ;
  Steady, my faithful Bess—to-ho—to-ho !
And even as I speak, the grey cock springs,
Bursts through the tangled brake, with whir of wings,
  And drops, dead bird, upon the heath below.
Once more, my mottled beauties, left and right,
Two well-directed shots have stopped your flight,
  The heart does penance, but the hand will kill ;
Good dog—dead bird—go seek,—dead bird, I say ;
  By Jove, another, and—another still ;
Steady, my braves, there's gallant sport to-day.
  And so, on rapid wings, the hours go by ;
  I little heed the moments as they fly ;
The covert we have beaten, o'er and o'er,
Have flushed a score of birds, at least, and more ;
  High noon is blazing on the purple crest ;

Call in the panting dogs, I fain would rest.
The fevered land lies throbbing in the heat;
    And I will seek some quiet cloister-shade,
    Some leafy mosque, with arabesque inlaid.
'Tis but a step to yonder still retreat,
    Where screens of silken canopies invite
    To cool siestas in the chastened light.
There are no frowning gates to bar the way;
    I hear no warder's challenge, as I pass;
    Latticed with leaves, and carpeted with grass,
Its sylvan doors are open to the day.
    I cross the threshold of this leaf-lined nest,
    And find myself at once a welcome guest.
No host receives me with a smiling face,
    But rare civilities have no surcease.
I am the sole possessor of the place,
    To break my bread and drink my wine in peace.
My dogs beside me, couched upon the sward,
I sit me down to lunch, like any lord.
    There is no sauce like appetite, I ween:
And I have dined and wined enough to be aware,
That brimming cups, and lengthy bills of fare
    Will not disperse the vapors of the spleen.
For while amid the salvos of the feast,
    A man may half forget his galling chain;
When'er this brief oblivion has ceased,
    There comes, as recompense, an afterpain.
And so, to fly the lure of tempting ills,
I take betimes to tent-life on the hills.
    There we obey the mandate, " Kill and eat,"
Because no meagre diet will suffice,
    When health and hunger by the camp-fire meet.
First, from the hanging haunch a tender slice,

Broiled on the glowing embers to a turn,
  And then impaled where blazing fagots burn,
A bird or two, by timely shot brought down,
Larded with bits of bacon, crisp and brown.
  What if the fare be plain, the service crude,
We have a wealth of appetite at least,
  And last of all, to cheer the solitude,
  A cup of camp-brewed coffee, amber-hued,
Which is the crowning glory of the feast.
  And then—at night, the song, the laugh, the jest,
  The camp-fire tales related with a zest:
How in the jungle some one chanced to meet
The shaggy monster, with the shuffling feet,
And how discretion sought a safe retreat.
  Hard, by the stream, beside the antlered oak,
The wolf, beneath my waistcoat, fast asleep,
  From my post-prandial pipe the coils of smoke
Unwind and vanish in the upper deep.
  Unmindful of the pendent sword, mayhap,
In dreamy lassitude, at ease I lie
  Upon the moorland's aromatic lap,
And scan the vast abyss of shoreless sky.

  Away, upon the outmost verge of sight,
  The livelong day, at that far height,
An eagle, resting on his wings,
Wheels round and round in circling rings.
  In pensive mood, I turn my half-closed eyes
Across the hazy lowlands, leagues away,
Where dim ethereal ramparts, vast and gray,
  Rise, Alps on Alps, against the vaulted skies.
I mark the splendid sweep of plain below,
  The miles on miles of undulating hills,

The darker gorges of the upland rills,
The sinuous curves where tree-fringed rivers flow.
  Mid-summer days have tanned the valley's hide,
  And draped the mountain's corrugated side
In dappled robes of gold and green and dun.
Where heat-waves wimple in the noonday sun,
  White farmsteads nestle under brooding trees,
  And gleam like white sails on the wrinkled seas.
Stout-hearted nomads, from far distant lands,
  Have pitched their tents, and lit their campfires
      here.
  And though the thirsty fields are brown and sere,
An ample harvest waits on willing hands.
  In all methinks I see the counterpart
  Of Italy, without her dower of art.
We have the lordly Alps, the fir-fringed hills,
The green and golden valleys veined with rills,
  A dead Vesuvius with its smoldering fire,
  A tawny Tiber sweeping to the sea.
  Our seasons have the same superb attire,
The same redundant wealth of flower and tree.
  Upon our peaks the same imperial dyes,
And day by day, serenely over all,
  The same successive months of smiling skies.
Conceive a cross, a tower, a convent wall,
  A broken column and a fallen fane,
  A chain of crumbling arches down the plain,
A group of brown-faced children by a stream,
  A scarlet-skirted maiden, standing near,
  A monk, a beggar, and a muleteer,
And lo, it is no longer now a dream.
  These are the Alps, and there the Apenines;
The fertile plains of Lombardy between;

83

Beyond, Val d'Arno with its flocks and vines;
These granite crags are gray monastic shrines,
Perched on the cliffs like old dismantled forts;
And far to seaward, can be dimly seen
The marble splendor of Venetian courts;
While one can all but hear the mournful rythmic
beat
Of white-lipped waves along the sea-paved street.
O childless mother of dead empires, we,
The latest born of all the western lands,
In fancied kinship stretch our infant hands
Across the intervening seas to thee.
Thine the immortal twilight, ours the dawn;
Yet we shall have our names to canonize,
Our past to haunt us with its solemn eyes,
Our ruins, when this restless age is gone.
Time was, whene'er the ardent sun rode by,
May blushed the while, and breathed a fragrant sigh.
Then came the passion of imperial June,
As morn is followed by the fervid noon,
And then the tawny splendor of July.
Metallic lustres brighten as the summer wanes.
The sky itself is like a sea of glass,
The snow-fed streams are links of silver chains,
The rounded hills are waves of molten brass.
Where erst the earth was clad in rainbow hues,
And gilded insects wraped themselves in fire;
Now Flora dies upon her kindled pyre,
And all the pagantry of death ensues.
In the still half-light of the nearer shade,
Where sunbeams filter through the leaves, behold!
The summer's pall, the autumn's masquerade,
The dead year's cast off garments turned to gold.

Here I escape the world's discordant noise,
    The burden of the nights which bring no rest;
    No palms appeal to me, no toilsome quest
For wealth or fame; in blissful equipoise,
    I lie content on nature's tranquil breast.
The calm repose of perfect peace abounds.
    I hear the breeze coquetting with the trees,
    The hum of myriad wings, the drone of bees,
And fill my heart with these delightful sounds.
    Lulled by the woodland's weird æolian lyre,
And the delicious babble of the streams,
I fold my listless hands, and dream my dreams,
    Unvexed by doubt, unruffled by desire.
No longer worldly wise, I hold a sweet
    Communion with the bee and bird and flower.
Speech fails and falters, when I would repeat
    The wondrous harmonies of this glad hour.
I know and only know, that as I kneel
    In silent ecstasy upon the sod,
I listen with my inmost soul, and feel
    No discords in the orchestras of God.
What though our aftermath be brown and sere,
I sound the pæan of the burgeoned year.
    The banners which at morn assailed the east,
Now trail in burnished pomp along the west.
    The vesper song of birds has well-nigh ceased,
And tranquil nature lulls herself to rest.
    Already twilight lurks within the wold,
So swift the hours have flown on silken wings.
    The waning daylight sows its dust of gold,
And on the crest a fitful splendor flings.
    As rapid hours complete the ripened day,
The new moon's sickle reaps the yellow sheaf.
    Whate'er betide of good or ill, alway
My book of life has one illumined leaf.

THE DEATH OF
AL HÂRITH

THE DEATH OF AL HÂRITH.

AL HAMADÂNI, wonder of his time,
Relates how Harith, blessed with goodly
    store,
The owner of a hundred steeds and more,
Grown overwise and restless in his prime
Set sail upon the desert seas of yore.
From Irak to Damascus, bold of wing,
He braves the tongue of flame, the simoon's blast;
Backward the iron hoofs of his coursers fling
The dust of travel, till he stands at last
Beside the blessed gate of Illah, where
The shining city sits beneath the palms.
His face towards Mecca first, he bows in prayer,
As all good Moslems should, bestows his alms,
And then betakes him to the bath ; then pays
His service to the Kadi, to express
With due decorum, all the grave excess
Of Oriental greeting ; length of days,
Increase of store—for thus, in Eastern lands,
With gracious speech, the Moslem greets his guest.
And so the son of Irak folds his hands,
And sits him down by Syrian streams to rest.
To Oriental ears no sound so sweet
As sound of running waters; while he makes
The pilgrimage of life in dust and heat,
He fondly hopes, whene'er his soul awakes
In Paradise, to realize his dreams
Of singing bulbuls and of babbling streams.

Damascus, gold within and grime without ;
With here and there a narrow tortuous street.
Through which the living tides flow in and out.

We catch a glimpse of palms above the walls,
And in the transient hush of hurrying feet,
We hear the tinkling tones of waterfalls.
Within the portals, sheltered from the heat,
When sultry days succeed to lustrous dawns,
Are cool arcades where shining waters run,
And tesselated courts, and terraced lawns,
And marble fountains, flashing in the sun.
'Twas much the same a thousand years ago.
The dreamy Moslem life pulsed to and fro
In the same sensual round, when Harith found
Its mosques and market places crescent-crowned.
A mart of splendor by a sea of sand,
Her khans were filled with wares from every land :
Spices and gums, frankincense, musk, and myrrh,
Amber and coral from the Indian seas ;
Brocades and arabesques from Nishampur,
Inwrought with gold and silver filigrees ;
Embroidered silks and satins, rare perfumes,
Rubies from Ava, pearls from Hindostan ;
Cambrics and tapestries from Persian looms,
Caftans from Fez, and shawls from Khorasan.
Rivers of wine and oil ran down her streets,
While, tossed and travel stained, the desert fleets,
With freights from Egypt, Khiva, and Cathay,
Beside her sacred gates at anchor lay.

Hot in the heart of youth ; what wonder, then,
As in his veins the streams of molten lava leap,
That he of Irak should, like other men,
Forget the words of wisdom, and despite
The warnings of the Prophet fall asleep
In some forbidden palace of delight ?

Meanwhile the moons of Syra waxed and waned;
And he, enchanted first and then enchained,
A willing slave in silken meshes lay,
Where broad-browed nymphs with sombrous waves
      of hair,
And lustrous eyes that shunned the light of day,
Like Venus veiled in phantom robes of spray,
Were idly swaying in the perfumed air.
Change follows change in all material things;
The dawn gives place to day, the day to night.
Our treasures, as the Prophet says, have wings,
And like the mists of morning take their flight.
Love tires of its delicious pain, and power
Is but the fleeting phantom of an hour.
Perhaps the still small voice, by night, was heard,
Which comes to us unbidden and unsought;
Perhaps the ghost of loves forsaken, stirred
Once more the turbid current of his thought.
If vows were made, or expiation done,
The text does not disclose, nor can we tell.
But this we know, he broke the Circean spell,
And swore by Allah that the morrow's sun
Should see him on his way: and when the dawn
With rosy fingers had in part withdrawn
The mantle of the night, he stole away,
Leaving the dancers at their revels still,
And with his camel drivers waited, till
The earth unveiled before the full-orbed day.
Beyond the gates, beside the sacred well,
In abject squalor on his leathern mat,
Abu Ben Zayd, the prince of beggars sat,
And told his wondrous tales, and sought to sell
His amulets: " This, from the holy shrine,

91

Will guard thee, son of Islam, from thy foes;
And this,—peace be with thee and thine,—
Will comfort thy distress, and soothe thy woes;
And this,—if thou shouldst chance to go astray,—
Will lead thee safely back." "Upon my word,"
Al Harith said, "I do believe
Thou liest; and as the spider weaves his web for prey,
So thou dost weave these pretexts to deceive."
The Prophet in the seventh heaven heard
The impious scoff, the dervish bowed his head:
   "Illah il' Allah!" God is great, he said.

A steel-blue sky above, and on either hand,
As far as the eye can reach, a sea of sand.
In all of the great white space no sound or sight;
Only the glare of day, only the hush of night.
Curses have followed like wolves, as they march
Day after day, under the arch
Of the pitiless sky; no joy and no rest,
For omens are thick in the thin white air;
And the camel-drivers forget to jest
When Fear looks into the face of Care.
In the door of his tent, Al Harith sits,
And his face wears a troubled look, for lo!
On the rim of the desert a shadow flits,
And it seems like the cloud of the coming foe.

   He hears their hoof-beats, nearer and more near;
   No hope in flight; and paralyzed with fear,
   He calls on Allah, but he calls in vain;
   Across the wide expanse of arid plain
   Full half a hundred horsemen dash;
   And foremost, where the circling sabres flash,

92

Behold! the face of him who sought to sell
The amulets beside the sacred well.

Ten centuries attest the force of this
One sabre stroke.
                In all the eastern lands
Abu Ben Zayd is held in high repute,
Because he fixed the faith in amulets,
And gave to every canting mendicant
From Mecca to Stamboul this poor pretext
To make a merchandise of piety.

    The Prophet says: "Give ear, O sons of men!
    Obey the precepts of the faith, and then
    Accept the preordained decrees of fate."
    "Illah il' Allah!" Only God is great.

DOM PERIGNON

DOM PERIGNON.

The Discoverer of Champagne.

CROSSING the purple hills of Epernay,
   Hard by the little thorp of Haut Villier,
   Just where the winding river blocks the way,
    A gray old ruin you may chance to see—
Long since the famous Abbey of Saint Pierre,
   But erst the castle keep of chivalry:
Where broad-arched portals led to columned courts,
   With terraces, and lawns, and blazoned halls,
And lists for jousts of arms, and manly sports;
   While, pendent from its battlemented walls,
The oriflamme of France flashed on the sight.
   Fresh from his conquests in the Holy Land,
His casque and corselet cast aside, the knight
   Bent here above his lady's jeweled hand:
And here, of old, did valiant men at arms
   Their wassails and their drinking bouts prolong
From dark till dawn;—instead of war's alarms,
   The gust of laughter and the gush of song.
Along these corridors their iron heels rang
   And here on festive nights, and tilting days,
His harp in hand the wandering minstrel sang
   His madrigals and tender roundelays.
Here, too, the jester in his cap and bells,
   With licensed leer, assailed pretense and sham—
Played carte and tierce with mediæval swells,
   And stabbed them with a well-turned epigram.
But knight, and minstrel, and my lady fair,
   Gave place to cowled monks. Some one has said:—
"The pen is mightier than the sword, and prayer
   More potent than the monarch's crown-ed head;"

And so it seems, for like a king of kings,
  The priest became the potentate of France—
Held court, and crown, and state in leading strings—
  Made war and peace, yet never lifted lance.

Who could foretell the change that was to be
  From rocky caves to grand cathedral aisles,
And from the manger to the Papal See?
  Beneath the domes of consecrated piles,
A treasure trove has been preserved for us—
  For music, marble, canvas could, in part,
Repeat the story of the Cross, and thus
  The Church became the very shrine of art.
At first, the monk could worship in his cell
  Without the ritual of form and cant;—
The burning taper and the tinkling bell,
  The swinging censor and the solemn chant.
He gave his life to prayer and holy thought;
  And when the enemy of souls enticed;
With scourge and fast, on bended knees, besought
  The Virgin Mother, and the risen Christ.
Not so our brotherhood of jovial fame;
  They ate with toothsome zest the rich repast—
Were bacchanals in fact, and monks in name,
  And loved the feast much better than the fast.
They cried: "Give us this day our daily bread,"
  Which meant fat capon for monastic greed;
And then they gathered tithes, waxed fat, and fed
  The hinds on husks of faith and crumbs of creed.
But who will dare to say they were not wise,
  If, for themselves, they killed the fatted calf?
  Not I, at least, for I have learned that half
  The fine-spun theories which men devise
  Are only snares, in short, for catching flies.

The monastery lands were deftly tilled—
   From year to year the Friars leased the soil,
Received therefore the lion's share, and filled
   The Abbey bins with corn and wine and oil.
Dom Perignon, purveyor of the vaults,
   With reputation reaching to our day—
   Like Sancho Panza's uncles, so they say —
Could tell at once the virtues and the faults
   Of every drop of wine produced ; and knew
   The kinds of grape, the hillsides where they grew,
   The modicum of sun and rain and dew,
With just the proper mixing to impart
   The flavor which the epicures require.
His brain, perhaps, was sluggish, but his heart
   Was like his wine, full of imprisoned fire.
   Who knows the fermentation of desire,
   Which fumed and fretted day and night, unseen,
   Beneath the Friar's unkempt gabardine ?

Some golden years gone by, ere youth had flown,
And ere youth's oaten follies had been sown,
   In that gay capital of La belle France,
It was my wont, at times, to stroll about
The haunts where madcap-students sing and shout,
   And where with gay grisettes they dance.
In an old cafe by the sluggish Seine,
Two close converging streets between,
Where these wild roisterers oft did congregate,
His portrait hangs, or there it hung of late.
In half a dozen dashes of the pen
   I'll try to sketch the likeness of the man—
   That is, I'll do the best I can ;
And if I fail, why then, what then ?

99

With some small share of tact, and less of art,
And more of that old Saxon gift called knack,
  As in charades, I'll improvise a part,
And dress it from my store of bric-a-brac.
  And first, the part most prominent, in fine,
  I'll take this Arab wine-skin filled with wine,
  And hang it here upon the smoky wall
  Above these Roman sandals; over all
  I'll drape this Friar's frowsy gown,
  And last, this masker's face—a full-orbed moon—
  And the sketch is done, from the shaven crown
  To the soles of the sandal-shoon.

Now, I'll be bound, you thought of course to see
  Some thin ascetic saint on prayers intent;
And not this counterfeit of piety.
  Small doubt, indeed, but he must needs repent—
In fact, but for his priestly robe, I fear
  He would be deemed an arrant sinner,
Far less concerned about his vows austere,
  Than for the flavor of his dinner.
But then, all men are prone to sin you know,
And monks, at best, are only men, and so
They wrap themselves in sackcloth, while they line
Their ample gowns with capon and with wine.
Concede, that to the priestly robe there clings
  An odor of sanctity, if you will,
We find that an angel without his wings
  Is only a mortal in dishabile.
A truce to dull polemics. You shall see,
  That not by constant prayer and self-restraint
  Did Padre Perignon become the saint
Of social Sybarites, like you and me.

But thus it came to pass one day
A cask of vapid Epernay,—
Which he, betimes, had fortified
  With syrup and with eau-de-vie,—
Made mad with effervescing pride,
  Burst its frail bonds exultingly.
Some drops fell on the Friar's lips,
His hand into the flood he dips,
And lo, a miricle! He sips
The drink divine, with wonder quaffs
A living wine that leaps and laughs.
Pale, phosphorescent spark, that lights
  A sensuous flame refined and rare—
All hail, O Monk! thy neophytes
  Are demigods—or think they are.
Look to thy laurels Bacchus! crown anew
  Thy cups with garlands, for thy wine has caught
A rarer spirit, and a richer hue,
  From this fat Friar's accidental thought.

We shed no hackneyed, ill-timed tears
  Upon an old monastic tomb;
But pour libations on a shrine.
  His name from out the cloistered gloom,
Borne on the tossing tide of wine,
  Drifts down the cycle of the years.
Amid the salvos of the feast,
Let all good bacchanals, at least,
In silence toast the jocund priest.

A REVERIE

A REVERIE.

I.

TURN back with me across the dim historic
    years,
    And pass the portals of the dark mysterious
      door,
Where pale-faced Sorrow sits beside the cairn in
    tears ;
Behold, the spectre of Imperial lust appears,—
  Its fleshless hands are red with human gore.

II.

Around this sombre silhouette softly plays
The mellow lustre of Castilian days.

On the long, low swell of the sleeping sea,
  At anchor a galleon swings at her chain.
On the strand a knight, on his bended knee,—
  In the sovereign name of Catholic Spain,—
Unfurls a standard loyally.
    Scarred veterans of elder lands,
    Their banners red, and red their hands,
    File rank on rank across the sands.
    So fair a sight was never seen ;
    Broad valleys, bound in gold and green,
    While stately rivers sweep between.

III.

    The pageant vanishes ; and in its place,
    A band of friars, in procession, climb
    The consecrated hill, with solemn face,
    And plant the emblem of their faith sublime.
    Where now they kneel upon the roofless sod,

Anon in minster walls they worship God.
Adown the summer silence I can hear
The silver chime of bells ring sweet and clear;
I see the vaulted nave, the surpliced priest,
The wine, the wafer, and the solemn feast,
The altar and the silvern candlesticks.
The carven Christ, the gilded crucifix,
The cups of beaten gold for sacred rites,
The smoking censor, and the waxen lights,
The sculptured saints, the dusky neophytes.

IV.

Time slowly weaves the web of fate,
Dynasties rise and fall:
And surely, soon or late,
Death comes to all.
Alike, beneath the sable pall,
The monarch and the monk lie down.
And so, his work of love and faith complete,
We see the good man calmly meet
The angel with the golden crown.

And while, methinks, I hear their sweet refrains
On every ripple of the ambient air,
The grass is growing in their fallen fanes,
    Their silver chimes no longer call to prayer.

V.

'Tis an o'er true tale, in the young New World,
Since that belted knight his banner unfurled,
His cross in the air, his keel on the main—
There's strife on the sea and toil on the plain,
For the white man's blood is the red man's bane.

Bronze statues of the mystic past,
I mark your slowly wasting lines,
Too crude in civic chains to last—
For you no promised morrow shines:
Victims of lawlessness and lust,
The end is certain, " dust to dust."

VI.

The years glide onward with noiseless feet,
  And the mystical seasons wax and wane,
Only prolonged by the summer's heat,
  Only defined by the winter's rain.
Before me stretches a pastoral land,
  Where the patriarch pitches his tent by the rills;
His corn land and vine land on either hand,
  And his flocks and his herds on a hundred hills.
When the hampers are filled with the fruits of the
     vine,
  And the sheaves of the reaper are garnered in,
Red from the wine-press flow rivers of wine,
  And the feasts of the autumn begin.
The young men laugh loud at their festive games,
  And the old men rejoice at the sight;
While the dark-eyed daughters of dark-browed dames
  Sing plaintive songs in the dusk of the night.

    O night of rest, O days of ease,
    In this the Garden of Hesperides;
    Here life was one long summer day;
    A day that never reaches noon—
    Where smiling May is always May,
    And roses bloom from June to June.

TRANSLATIONS

SERENADE.

From the French of Theophile Gautier.

I WOULD climb to where she stands,
  Looking down with parted lips;
But alas, my outstretched hands
  Cannot touch her finger tips.

Bid thy old duenna leave,
  Drop thy silken girdle, sweet;
Or a ladder deftly weave
  From thy lute-strings, for my feet.

Loose thy comb, discard the rose,
  Lean, until the tawny hair,
Which round about thee flows,
  Makes for me a magic stair.

Quickly then to thee above,
  Will thy lover lightly rise;
He, though not an angel, love,
  Knows the way to paradise.

III

ROSETTE.

After Beranger.

I N THIS, the heyday of your youth,
   How can you sit and prate, my dear,
Of love and faith to one, forsooth,
   Whose forty years are in the sear?
Time was, when my fond heart could pay
   Its vows to one obscure grisette;
Ah, me! if only I, to-day,
   Could love you as I loved Rosette.

Your grand equipage serves to show
   The silks and diamonds which you wear;
Rosette, Rosette, her cheeks aglow,
   Tripped by with roses in her hair.
Her eyes, despite my jealous " Nay,"
   Provoked a word from all we met;
Ah, me! if only I, to-day,
   Could love you as I love Rosette.

In your boudoir, with satin lined,
   The mirrors show your smiling face;
In her wee glass, I used to find
   The image of a new-born Grace.
No curtains barred the morning ray,
   And stars peeped in when sun had set;
Ah, me! if only I, to-day,
   Could love you as I loved Rosette.

Your wit and fancy flash, until
   The poet's heart is somehow stirred;
I do not blush to own it, still
   Rosette could scarcely read a word.

Her simple speech sufficed, alway,
　To tell her love, and yet, and yet,
Ah, me ! if only I, to-day,
　Could love you as I loved Rosette.

Her charms were less than yours, God wot,
　She may have loved me more, although,
I must confess her eyes had not
　The fire of passion yours can show ;
But then she had, I fain must say,
　My youth, which I perhaps regret ;
Ah, me ! if only I, to-day,
　Could love you as I loved Rosette.

♣

CARMEN.

From the French of Theophile Gautier.

DARK rings encircle her gypsy eyes,
　And her figure is scrawny and thin ;
Her hair is black as the midnight skies,
　And the devil has tanned her skin.

Men rave about her, but women swear
　She is ugly as ugly can be ;
They even hint in Toledo there,
　That the bishop chants mass at her knee.

Her piquant plainness may have, who knows ?
　A grain of salt from the self-same seas,
Whence nude, erewhile, to the crest she rose,
　A racy Venus to tempt and tease.

113

TO.............

From the Polish of Wladyslaw Syrokomla.

COME down from your palace, my dear;
   Bring the gauds and the garments you
     wear;
I have little to offer you here,
Save a shrine that is empty and bare.

But you come not, my lady, to fast;
   Your lover will watch lest you pine;
He will serve you a royal repast,
   And feast you on sentiment fine.

You shall breakfast on roses ere long;
   And dine on the murmur of streams,
And sup on the nightingale's song,
   And revel all night in sweet dreams.

And if, to the star-studded skies,
   You would soar on your pinions, my love,
Through the rents in my roof your rapt eyes
   May gaze on the heavens above.

REMEMBRANCE.

From the German of Heine.

WHAT wilt thou mournful vision dear and
olden?
I feel thy very breath and gaze on thee;
I am by thee with doleful eyes beholden;
I know thee, and alas, thou knowest me.

I am a way-worn man, my limbs a-weary
Have lost their strength, my heart is scorched
and sere;
Care weighs me down, my days are dark and dreary;
It was not thus when first I found thee here.

In haughty strength I left the home seclusion
To tramp the wide world o'er, and would assault
The gates celestial, in my mad delusion,
And tear the very stars from Heaven's vault.

Frankfort doth foster fools and knaves, I know it,
And yet she gave, for this I love her well,
Many good Kaisers, and our greatest poet;
And there I found my love where she did dwell.

I strolled along the Ziel amid the bustle;
There was a fair, with all its fuss and feud;
The motley throng went by with rush and rustle,
And I looked idly on in dreaming mood.

I saw her there, with shy delighted wonder,
And watched her swaying form that self-same
hour;
Her happy eyes, the long dark lashes under,
Attracted me with such unwonted power,

115

Through street and market then I followed after,
  Until we reached a cottage by and by,
The sweet one turned and with a flash of laughter,
  She slipped into the house, and so did I.

The aunt was vile, would even sell for money,
  This maiden flower that bloomed so sweetly there ;
Although the child gave me herself, so sunny,
  Without a single sordid thought, I swear.

I have met other women than the Muses,
  And know the varnished face, the artful sigh ;
Hers was no breast to heave whene'er it chooses,
  And in her eyes, by Heaven, there was no lie.

And she was fair, far fairer than is painted
  That foam-begotten Goddess of the sea :
Perchance she was the being well-nigh sainted ;
  Who in my boyhood's dreams appeared to me.

I knew it not, and it was all unheeded,
  Some spell entranced me with, I know not what ;
Perchance the bliss I longed for and most needed
  Was in my arms and yet I knew it not.

And she was fair, far fairer in her anguish,
  When after three days' blissful dream I fain
Would leave the heart I rested on to languish,
  Because the old mood drove me forth again.

With her dishevelled hair about her flying,
  And mute and wild appeals her hands she wrung ;
Then at my feet she cast herself and lying,
  Burst into tears as to my knees she clung.

Ah God! her blood, would I had seen it never,
  My spur had caught her hair upon the floor;
I tore myself away and lost forever
  My darling child, and never saw her more.

The mood is gone, upon her face I ponder,
  That face, where'er I am, appears to me;
Poor child! in what cold desert dost thou wander
  With want and misery,—my gifts to thee?

♣

DEDANS PARIS.

Clement Marot, 1497-1544.

I N PARIS there, brave city, where
    I wandered once, weighed down with care,
    Until I met, by chance, one day,
    A blithe Italian maid so gay,
  With whom no maiden can compare.

  She hath a modest mien and air,
  Her truthful eyes are not a snare—
    Whatever others do or say
        In Paris there.

  We sealed our friendship sweet and rare,
  With just one guileless kiss, I swear;
    Her name I never will betray,
    Enough to know, that she alway
  Is my fast friend, come foul or fair;
        In Paris there.

LET THEM DREAM.

From the German.

AND the ghost of midnight, side by side,
   Stalk up and down these silent streets at
     will;
How short a time since here men laughed
   and cried—
One little hour ago, now all is still.
Erewhile joy vanished like a cast-off flower;
   The empty goblet lies beside the stream;
Pale sorrow hid away at twilight hour;
   The world is tired, so let it, let it dream.

My hate has ceased, my wrath has taken flight,
   As when at ease the storm-clouds break awhile,
The peaceful moon looks down with tender light,
   And gilds the withered roses with her smile.
I walk these silent streets with bated breath,
   I hold communion with myself; it seems
My soul would almost search the realm of death
   To solve the mystery of human dreams.

My shadow trails behind me like a thief—
   Before the gloomy prison bars I stand—
Thy faithful son, in bitter, bitter grief,
   Atones his love for thee, O Fatherland!
He sleeps and dreams—what chains can bind him
   now?—
   Dreams of a hamlet by the wooded stream;
Dreams that the victor's crown is on his brow;
   O God of Justice, let the captive dream!

Before me towers the lofty castle keep;
   Between the purple curtains I can see
118

The startled Cæsar clutch his sword in sleep,
  And shudder as he dreams of treachery.
He mutters to himself, and shrinks with fright;
  His pallid face is plowed with many a seam;
A thousand steeds are saddled for his flight;
  O God of Vengeance, let the despot dream!

The cottage by the brook, how small it seems;
  Yet want and worth together share one bed.
The Lord will let his vassal dream his dreams—
  Such fancies serve to calm his waking dread.
When slumber's silken meshes are unfurled,
  He sees his ample cornfields' golden gleam,
His narrow homestead widens to the world;
  O God of Mercy, let the poor man dream!

In yonder house, upon a bench of stone,
  A blessing will I carve, and rest from care;
I love thee well, my child, though not alone—
  My heart with Freedom you must ever share.
You dream of turtle-doves and butterflies,
  While I can only hear the eagle's scream;
Can only see my war-steed's flashing eyes;
  O God, I pray thee, let my darling dream!

O stars, that from the clouds like fortune break!
  O night, that folds us in thy soft embrace!
Let not the sleeping world too soon awake,
  To gaze upon my grief-disfigured face.
Not yet can baffled Liberty afford
  To light her camp-fires by the day's broad beam,
Lest tyranny again should whet her sword;
  O God of Slumber, let the sleepers dream!

CHILDE HAROLD.

From the German of Heine.

NOW black and stark, a stately bark,
 Bears calmly on with canvass spread;
In silence all, around a pall,
 The watches watch beside the dead.

A poet dies, and calm he lies,
 His face uncovered to the sight;
His eyes of blue cerulean hue,
 Fixed on the far celestial light.

From out the deep, tones swell and sweep,
 Such as the moaning mermaids make;
With ceaseless surge, like solemn dirge,
 Against the bark the billows break.

❧

SONG.

Translated from the German of Heine.

AT THE dawn I rise and query,
 " Comes my love to-day? "
In the dusk I moan aweary,
 " She remained away."

All the night, with my sore sorrow,
 Sleepless here I lie.
Half asleep, when comes the morrow,
 Dreaming, wander I.

FROM THE BARRICADES.

After Heine.

POETS sleep and dream no more,
Wake to deeds of high emprise,
Strike the chords of lute and lyre
Till they fill the soul with fire,
Like the Marseillaise of yore.

Pipe no more in accents weak
To your lady's love lit eyes;
A la bayonett the word,
On the ramparts it is heard,
Let the swords and daggers speak!

Suffer not your lute to trill
Softly in idyllic sighs;
Be a trumpet in its call,
Be a cannon charged with ball,—
Peal and thunder, roar and kill.

Peal and roar as days go by,
Till the last oppressor dies;
And until the world is free,
Let your song from henceforth be
One exultant battle cry.

SO HERE THEN ENDETH ON THE HEIGHTS: A VOLUME OF VERSE, BY LUCIUS HARWOOD FOOTE, AS DONE INTO A BOOK BY ME, ELBERT HUBBARD, AT THE ROYCROFT SHOP, WHICH IS IN EAST AURORA, N. Y., U. S. A., AND COMPLETED THIS TENTH DAY OF SEPTEMBER, MDCCCXCVII

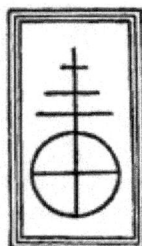

ERRATA.

Contents,—for "De Profundus" read "De Profundis."

Page 25, 4th line, after "How" insert "the."

" 30, for "De Profundus" read "De Profundis."

" 36, 7th line from bottom, omit "with."

" 39, 9th line from bottom, for "Hairi" read "Hariri."

" 41, 9th line, from bottom, for "por" read "port."

" 42, 7th line, for "were" read "was "

" 43, 2d line, for "balm" read "balms."

" 44, 7th line, for "How" read "Now."

" 53, 3d line, for "cliffs" read "clefts."

" 54, for "El Salvadore" read "El Salvador."

" 58, 1st line, for "of" read "in."

" 60, 2d line, before "serfdom" insert "the."

" 67, 2d line from bottom, for "gleaning peaks" read "gleaming pikes."

" 76, 10th line, for "exalt" read "exult."

" 78, 4th line, for "on tides" read "on the tides."

" 79, 20th line, for "and lichens" read "the lichens."

" 80, 1st line, for "lips" read "lip."

" 90, 6th line, from bottom, for "Hot in" read "Hot is."

" 91, 1st line, for "Syra" read "Syria."

" 111, 6th line from bottom, for "round about" read "around about."

" 120, 4th line, for "watches" read "watchers."

"ON THE HEIGHTS"

A Review of the Collected Poems of Lucius H. Foote.

The prominence of individual literateurs is determined largely by environment. A writer who is proclaimed a great man in New York is great for America, whereas the fame of a distinguished San Franciscan is bounded by California. There has been a huge critical outcry over the publication in book form of certain poetical writings of Edmund Clarence Steadman, whose celebrity is a New York creation. The dailies are full of choice extracts and agreeable commendation. Yet Mr. Steadman's vogue is, in a degree, a fashion. He is the proper literary thing, and one bows to his verse when it appears as irreproachable poetry. I question whether the verdict of the English critics, who may not be aware of Mr. Steadman's importance, will fall—in with this chorus. It is highly probable they will admit the correctness of manner, but will ask the wherefore of all the enthusiasm. Contemporaneous with the issuance of this volume appears, unheralded, a collection of the verse of Lucius Harwood Foote—a San Franciscan whose writings are not unknown to readers of *The Wave*. Yet in regions where the personality of Steadman carries no weight, there will be compliments and recognition for Foote which the poems of the former cannot command.

There are many charming and graceful poems in *On the Heights*. The writer is most punctilious in his regard for form and diction. His inspiration is drawn from a variety of sources—here are lyrics, sonnets, ballads and ballades, in innumerable styles and metres, characterized by simplicity invariably, and by real excellence of versification. What is better than a mastery of manner, however, is the sense of poetic feeling which is manifest throughout this volume. In such brief snatches as "Waiting," "The Wooing of the Rose," "Marie," "De Profundis," "Summer Days," there is the veritable touch, a breath of the magic that is poetry. Trailing through each of these graceful poems are the delicate threads of a story—the mere suggestion of an incident exquisitely wrought in. I have ventured to reproduce some of these—many of the others were published when written—"Guido," for instance, "Richard Lovelace," and "Lady Jane," in which there is the antique ballad flavor. "Types," too, is admirable. How many writers of the day are doing better than this:

Though her marvelous face, with its halo of hair,
Is so hauntingly fair,
There's a smoldering fire which flickers and flashes
Beneath her lashes,
And the ghost of an old Patrician disdain,
Like the phantom of pain,
Is lurking now
In the swell of her nostril, and shade of her brow.
In fine.

There is pride and passion in every line,
From her finger tips,
To the arch of her foot, and the curve of her lips.
Men have gone to their death, for women like this,
And counted it bliss.
In the hush of her chamber, this very night,
She will tell her beads in the chastened light,
And pray to the Mother of God to keep
Her soul in sleep.

"The Hymn," "To the Unknown God" a poem that will undoubtedly attract in this form some of the attention its inspiration deserves. It is a notably fine flight, written in a metre that conveys the strenuous "pulse of automatic vibrations." The translations are especially clever. There are several from the French of Gautier, and the German of Heine that are delightfully dainty and felicitous. Indeed, *On the Heights* is certainly a volume that will give real pleasure to the lover of poetry, and I predict for it an unusual degree of critical consideration. The typography of the volume is admirable—like other products of the Roycroft Printing shop. However, here follow certain of General Foote's briefer poems. That on the Sacramento is the fifth verse of a charming poem, for all of which there is not space. The rest tell their own story.